THE ILLUSTRATED
MOTORCYCLE LEGENDS

ROY BACON

CHARTWELL
BOOKS, INC.

Previous page: The 1971 A65FS Firebird Scrambler.

Acknowledgements

The author and publishers wish to acknowledge their debt to all who loaned
material and photographs for this book. Many came from the extensive collection
of old friend Dick Lewis, whose Weybridge firm served the needs of BSA owners
for over a century. Other sources were *Motor Cycle News*, courtesy of the editor,
EMAP, whose archives hold the old *Motor Cycle Weekly* files, the Mick Woollett
archive, the AA, who used the side-valve model for so many years, Californian
friend Art Sirota and friend Don Mitchell, who kindly loaned material from his
extensive stock. Other material came from the author's own files, collected over
the years. Thanks to all who helped.

Published by
CHARTWELL BOOKS, INC.
A division of **BOOK SALES, INC.**
P.O. Box 7100
Edison, New Jersey 088 18-7100

ISBN 0 7858 0254 1

Designed by Anthony Cohen

Printed and bound in China

CONTENTS

BICYCLE START

BSA - whose 'Piled Arms' trademark signified their Birmingham Small Arms origins as suppliers of rifles to the British government. Founded in 1861, BSA made guns by machines rather than crafted by hand,which gave them invaluable experience in precision, mass-produced metalwork.

Such expertise served them well when they entered the bicycle business around 1880, and this led to their supplying parts to the infant motorcycle trade. From these parts others built complete machines as early as 1904, either as a heavy-duty bicycle with a Minerva engine hung from its downtube, or with the frame amended to take the engine upright.

After a demonstration ride on the boardroom table by Mr. Otto, BSA began building this Dicycle in 1880.

By 1884 BSA had turned to this safety bicycle, using scrap gun parts in its construction.

BSA soon became a major cycle firm. This is a gent's model from the 1917 catalogue.

In 1904 the firm began to offer frames and other components to take an engine. This is a Belgian Minerva.

An alternative 1904 design of frame to take an upright engine.

FIRST MODEL AND WAR

It was not until October 1910 that BSA announced their first production motorcycle, one that reflected their approach of avoiding the extreme or radical, but offering good design, the best in materials and finish, reliability and the right price. It was a policy that stood them in good stead for many years and they prospered while they kept to it.

That first BSA was an excellent example of good practice of the time. The 3½hp engine was of 85 x 85mm and 499cc, with side valves and a chain-driven magneto ahead of it. It was mounted vertically in the frame which had spring forks, a Brooks saddle and good detailing. Direct belt drive from an adjustable engine pulley was used, a hub clutch being an option.

Variations were soon added in the form of a two-speed hub and a TT model, these being joined in 1914 by a 4¼hp sidecar model of 556cc, achieved by extending the stroke. Listed as the model H, it had a three-speed gearbox and all-chain drive, taking over as the mainstay of the range when the Great War broke out. Only the TT version of the 3½hp continued, but the H was joined by the model K, which had belt final drive. These, along with a vast arsenal of armaments, kept BSA busy for the duration of the First World War.

This single-speed model is from 1913, but little altered from the first one of 1910.

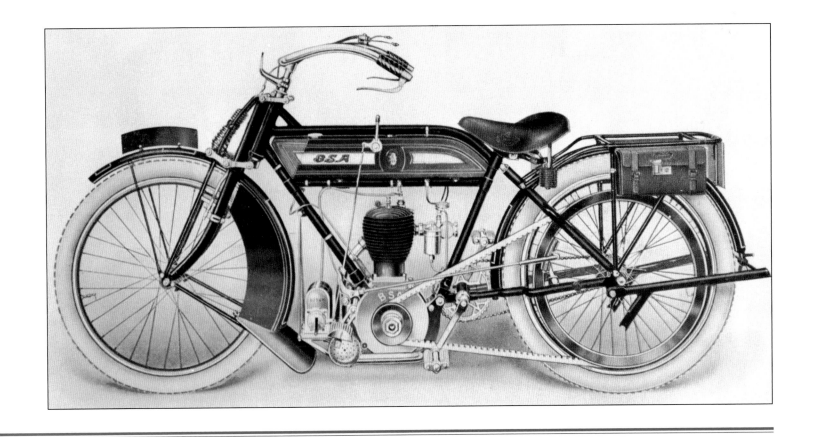

All 1913 models had a 3½hp engine, this the two-speeder with belt drive.

By 1913 BSA also produced an all-chain-drive, two-speed model, the chains fully enclosed in cases.

Production continued during WW1, by which time the 4¼hp model H with all-chain drive had joined the range.

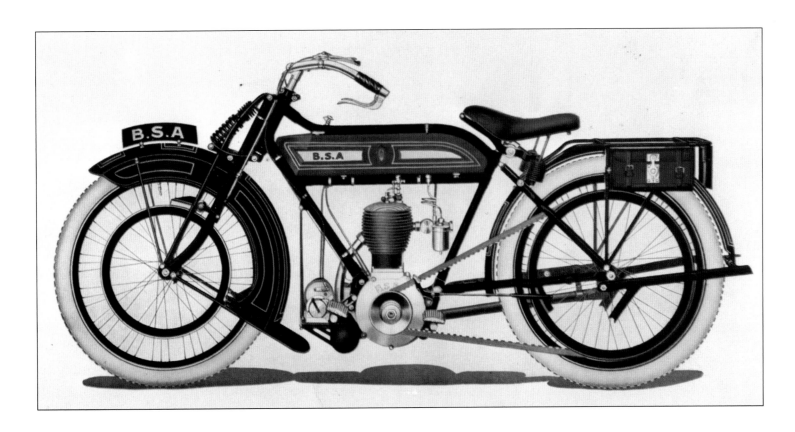

Only the TT version of the 3½hp machine continued after 1914. Listed as the model D, it had direct belt drive.

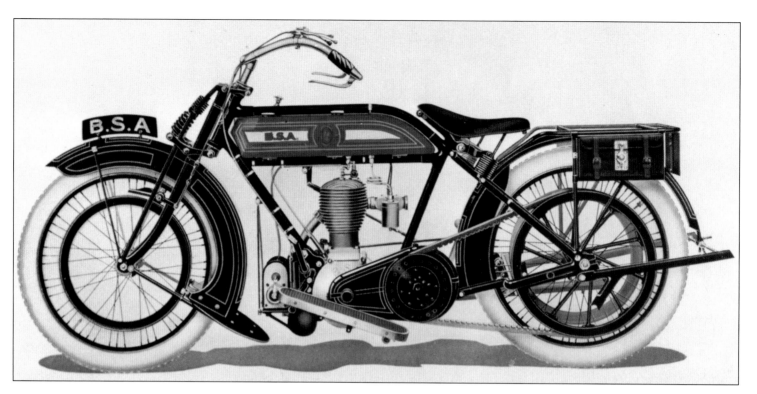

Above: The larger 4¼hp model was listed as the model K with belt final drive, hardly an asset in Flanders' mud.

Right: Neat drawing from a wartime brochure to depict the main role of the motorcycle in the conflict.

A wartime situation involving BSAs, their riders either map reading or lost!

BSA offered sidecars for their machines, such as this one from 1916.

V-TWIN AND OHV

Anew model was added for 1920, the E with a 6-7hp V-twin engine of 76 x 85mm and 771cc. It had a magneto at the front, three-speed gearbox, both drive chains enclosed by cases, and set a pattern of BSA twins which lasted until 1940. That 1920 year was the last for the 3½hp TT model, while 1921 saw the chaincase material altered to alloy. This was also the year that the factory suffered a disaster at the Isle of Man TT race, all their works entries retiring - a debacle that kept them out of racing for a very long time.

The range was extended for 1922 to add a larger V-twin for sidecar use, the model F of 985cc and 8hp, which became the model G for 1924. Before then, for 1923, two new singles joined the list - the 348cc L and the 493cc S, both conventional side-valve singles with three-speed gearboxes. For 1924, the last year of the belt-drive K, two important new models were added, the B and the ohv L.

Both broke new ground. The B was a low-price machine with a 249cc engine, two-speed gearbox, brakes on the rear wheel only and a cylindrical petrol tank which gave rise to its 'Round Tank' nickname. It sold well, for it offered the simple, reliable, basic transport the public wanted and by 1926 was also listed in de luxe form with three speeds. The new L kept to the 348cc capacity but introduced overhead valves for the first time on a production BSA.

For the next two years the basic range stayed as it was but added extra versions

After the war BSA added the V-twin, 771cc model E to its range for sidecar duty, a model type which ran for two decades.

that were cheaper, de luxe or for colonial use. Then, in 1927, another BSA legend appeared - the Sloper, which had its 493cc engine fitted with overhead valves and inclined in the frame. It offered good performance combined with quiet running and a low saddle height style, so sold well.

The firm's next venture was their first model to be fitted with a two-stroke engine of 174cc, its two-speed gearbox being built in unit. The frame comprised tubes bolted together and both brakes operated in the rear hub, so construction was very simple. Listed as the model A from 1928 to 1930, it was not a success, even when a third speed was added to the gearbox.

There were changes for 1929, as all models, except the G, went over to a saddle petrol tank and more machines with their engines inclined, Sloper style, were added. These included a short-lived Dirt Track, or speedway, model and several sizes of both side and ohv engines. Tuned versions of the Sloper engine became available and these had a red star stencilled on the timing case to distinguish them - the start of the star models which were to come later.

Model H as in 1920, complete with its fully-enclosed chains.

The model K was also offered in 1920 for those who preferred belt drive. It was quiet and flexible but prone to slip in the wet.

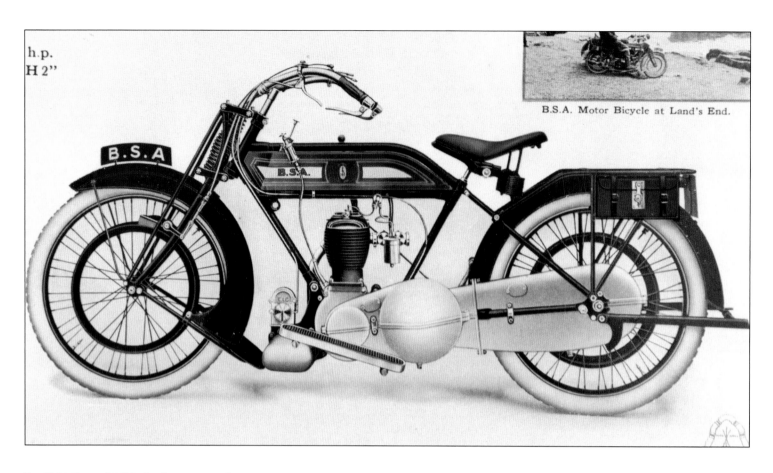

h.p.
H 2"

B.S.A. Motor Bicycle at Land's End.

For 1921 the model H had a fine new set of alloy chaincases and became the H2.

h.p.
"K 2"

B.S.A. Motor Bicycle at French Headquart

The model K copied the H2, but with just the front case to become the K2

In 1921 BSA entered the Senior TT with a team of machines, but all retired.

One of the sidecars listed for 1921, a time when passengers had to be as hardy as the rider.

Although known as the model E, the first twin was listed as the model A early on as here in 1921.

The first overhead-valve BSA was this 1924 model L of 348cc capacity.

Typical rider and BSA side-valve single of the early 1920s.

The motorcycle taxi appeared in 1920 to meet a demand, and this is a restored 1924 model powered by the V-twin

Famous 1924 model B, best known as the 'Round tank' but also as the 'Flying marrow' due to the colour.

Colonial versions of most models were available. This is a 1925 G, which has been modified to improve off-road capabilities.

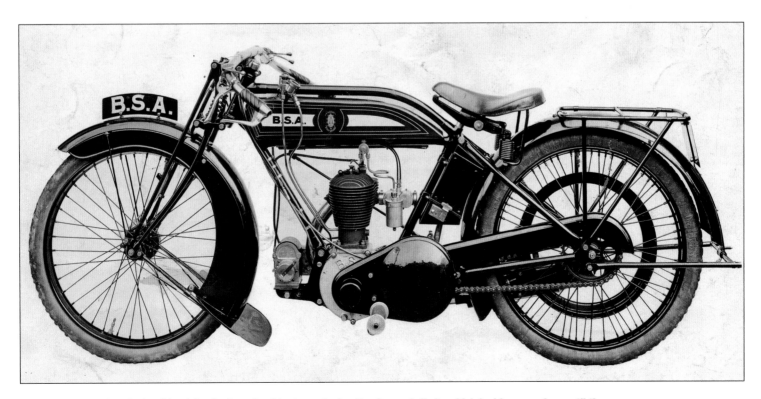

Mid-1920s side-valve single with miniscule drum front brake replacing the dummy belt-rim which had been used up until then and is still in use here on the rear wheel.

Above: In 1926 two Colonial model G outfits set out on a two-year tour around the world to promote the firm. They are seen here in Bombay.

This 1961 picture shows a 1926 side-valve BSA in Colombo where it was still giving its owner good service.

Long before the postwar Bantam, the GPO was using BSA machines on post rounds. This is a 348cc model L pictured at Evesham.

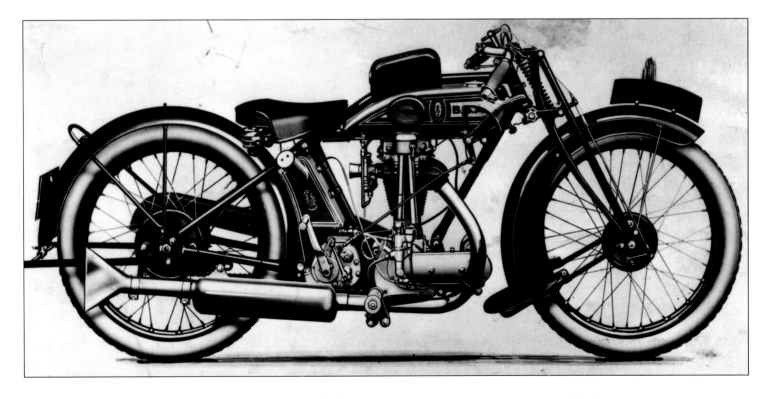

The ohv model L was also listed as the Super Sports, and this 1928 version is in race trim, hence the tank pad and fishtail exhaust.

BSA's first two-stroke powered model was this 1928 model A which was not to be a success.

Sturdy and reliable was what BSA was all about, as exemplified by this model H from the late 1920s.

Nancy Debenham and her sister Betty were BSA competition riders in the 1920s, bringing much publicity to the firm. This machine is a 1927 model B.

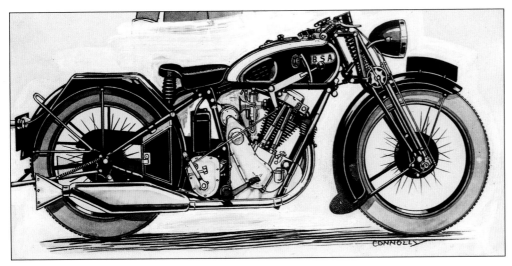

The famous Sloper model S whose inclined 493cc engine began a trend. This is a 1929 version.

The side-valve single followed the inclined-engine trend, at first as the 493cc S, later enlarged to 596cc, this a 1935 version.

DEPRESSED YEARS

Then came the 1930s - the depression years - and the inclined engine proved to be a short-lived fashion. Both it and the upright remained available as the firm desperately sought any and all sales, but in time the vertical style took over. As the depression ebbed, BSA began to offer a little more than basic transport, starting with the Blue Star ohv singles in 1932, the year that 499cc engines took over from the older 493cc type. More Blue Stars, along with tuned Specials were introduced for the next year when the 348cc engine was revised and the 556cc one stretched out to 596cc and offered in side and ohv form.

The revised range had lost the old 771cc V-twin after 1931, but for 1934 gained the model J which had been developed for service use and had a 499cc, ohv, V-twin engine. It was joined by a neat 149cc ohv single, the model X, and for one year only, the model FF, a 499cc machine with a fluid flywheel and preselector gearbox. It was an interesting project but the gearbox limited the performance too much for the model to appeal.

Up until 1936 little changed. That year saw the 596cc ohv model dropped from the range, but its slot was filled by the model Y, which had a 748cc, ohv, V-twin engine similar to the J. At the year end a major range revision took place to simplify the design which had become too varied for economic production.

For 1930 an ohv 249cc model B was added to the range, a typical product of the hard times.

The big V-twin as sold through the 1930s, during which time it altered little. This is as for 1935.

Above: Mrs Vera Harding-Foster about to try out a 1934 Sloper, which is still on trade plates.

B.S.A. 3.48 h.p. O.H.V. Blue Star £57.10s.

Model R35-5

Price includes electric equipment and licence holder

Upswept exhaust pipes and an improved performance created the Blue Star models. This is the smaller 348cc version in 1935.

For three years BSA listed a 596cc ohv model with an inclined engine. 1935 was its final year.

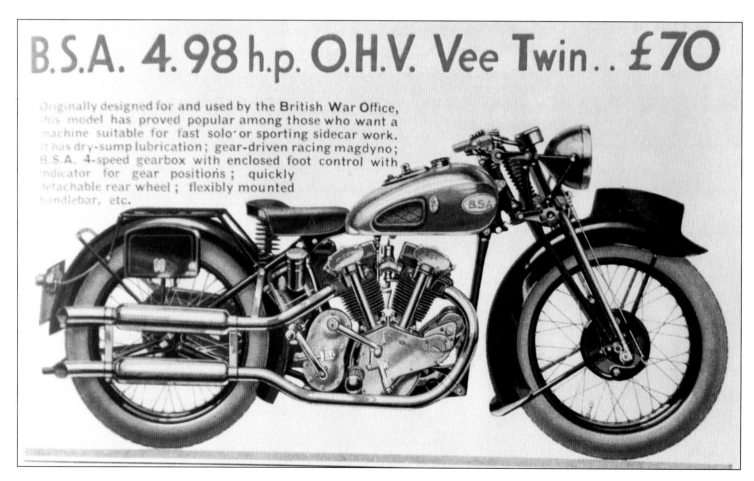

B.S.A. 4.98 h.p. O.H.V. Vee Twin.. £70

Originally designed for and used by the British War Office, this model has proved popular among those who want a machine suitable for fast solo or sporting sidecar work. It has dry-sump lubrication; gear-driven racing magdyno; B.S.A. 4-speed gearbox with enclosed foot control with indicator for gear positions; quickly detachable rear wheel; flexibly mounted handlebar, etc.

First built for the army, the 499cc V-twin model J was listed for three years from 1934-1936.

The 149cc model X fitted a road tax bracket and followed the lines of other ohv BSA models.

B.S.A. 4.99 h.p. O.H.V.
MOTOR CYCLE
WITH DAIMLER
FLUID FLYWHEEL
TRANSMISSION
Equipped ready for the road
with Electric Lighting, Electric
Horn and Licence Holder.

£79

BSA showed this model using a Daimler fluid flywheel and pre-selector three-speed gearbox late in 1933. Few were built as it was expensive and the oil drag ruined the performance.

Very basic 1935 249cc side-valve single. Typical BSA and tough enough to stand much abuse on the daily grind to work

Sporty 348cc de luxe single whose pushrod enclosure suggests ohc rather than ohv.

The 249cc ohv model retained the two pushrod tubes and offered close to 60mph, a useful performance for the mid-1930s.

Above: For sidecar work BSA listed this 499cc side-valve model, well able to trundle along all day at its modest pace.

Standard ohv 499cc model which served solo and sidecar riders equally well.

One of the mid-1930s sidecars listed by BSA, this the Special Sports single-seater listed in two-tone blue or green and ivory.

Enlarged ohv twin, the 1936 model Y of 748cc was very similar to the smaller J.

BSA listed competition versions of their models, such as this 1936 348cc R19, suitably amended.

THE PAGE LINE

The man responsible for the new 1937 range was Val Page, and his brilliant work was to remain in production into the 1960s. The 150 was dropped and, of the V-twins, only the 748cc ohv and 985cc sv were retained. Page concentrated his new design into just two machine ranges, the light B and the heavier M. Both used the same form of engine construction with a rear-mounted magneto driven by gears and dry-sump lubrication, and they were robust and reliable.

Both 249 and 348cc engines with side or overhead valves were used by the B range, the sports models listed as Empire Stars and one ohv 350 as a Competition model. The M range included one ohv of 349cc, side-valve models of 496 and 596cc, and standard and Empire Star versions using the 496cc ohv engine.

For 1938 the largest side-valve single was amended to 591cc and two new models were added, both important. The prosaic one was the C10, very simple and basic, using a 249cc, side-valve engine with coil ignition. The other was developed from the Empire Star and listed as the M24 but became far better known as the Gold Star from the performance of a tuned model at the Brooklands track. It had an all-alloy, bench-tested engine, and other sports features, and was also listed in competition and track racing forms.

In 1938 BSA made an attempt to gain the Maudes Trophy, awarded for demonstrations of reliability on the road, and succeeded after an arduous test.

Their C range grew in 1939 with the addition of the 249cc ohv C11, while the

The side-valve sidecar machines became the 496cc M20 and 596cc M21, both of which were to have a long life.

An Empire Star, B-range model, either a 249cc B22 or 348cc B24, which shared the same basic engine, this one in the optional red finish of 1938.

Empire Star models were replaced by Silver Stars, but only in 348 and 496cc sizes. The 748cc V-twin was dropped but the venerable model G continued, still showing its 1920s roots. Changes were scheduled for 1940, among them a 348cc, side valve C12 and the B29 of the same size, this based on the M-engine crankcase with fully-enclosed, overhead-valve springs. Only a handful of 1940 models were built before war broke out, but the B29 was to lead on to a postwar series.

During the conflict BSA again produced a great quantity of ordinance, along with large numbers of motorcycles. The bulk of these were the side-valve 496cc M20s, but there were C10s for training and some C11s for India. The firm did not think the M20 was the best option for the services, although it was tough and reliable, and proposed something better. The outcome was the WB30, which was based on the B29, and a small batch were built. Alas, the next major order was amended to M20s, then came the blitz and the new model was shelved but not forgotten.

Top of the new range for 1937 was the M23 Empire Star but all M-models had a similar line.

Simple and cheap, the 1938 249cc C10 provided transport for utilitarian duties.

COMPLETE SHOW REPORT No. 1857 Vol. 61 3ᴰ

THE MOTORCYCLE

B.S.A GOLD STAR

Right throughout
every model in the
B.S.A range is FIRST
in its class

Write for Motor Cycling Annual B.S.A. CYCLES LTD.,

STAND 12, Earls Court, Nov. 7th to 12th

The M24 Gold Star was the super sports model for 1938, and had an all-alloy, bench-tested 499cc engine.

Rare, restored competition version of the Gold Star as seen at the Classic Bike show in 1992.

The ohv 249cc C11 was added for 1939, both C-range models having the oil and petrol tanks as one.

It might have been a world beater: A B.S.A. o.h.c. vertical twin five-hundred built in 1938-9. Joe Craig worked on this engine, which was capable of 100 m.p.h. before development stopped

One of two prewar prototype twins built in 1938-39, this one with ohc and a 100mph potential, but neither was to be seen again.

Wartime scooter prototype, the Dinghy, ridden here by Graham Walker, father of Murray.

The M20 was the mainstay of BSA wartime motorcycle production, along with many armaments.

AUSTERITY AND EXPANSION

After the war BSA announced a four-model range for 1946, which comprised the C10, C11 and M20 virtually as in 1939, with a fourth machine listed as the B31. Based on the stillborn B29, it kept the M-type crankcase and enclosed valve gear, but featured telescopic front forks which were to serve the firm well.

The range soon began to expand, the 591cc M21 being added early in 1946, quickly followed by the B32, a competition version of the B31 with off-road tyres and much more chrome-plating. During that Spring both C models changed to telescopic front forks, and late in the year BSA announced a new vertical twin, the A7, of the type which became common in the British industry from then on. Of 495cc capacity, it was conventional enough, its cycle parts very similar to those of the larger singles.

At the start of 1947 the range was joined by the B33, a 499cc version of the B31, and a few months later a B34 competition model followed it. A further variation was created for 1948 by slotting the 499cc ohv engine into the heavy-duty M frame to create the M33, intended for the sidecar driver. That year also brought the first of one of BSA's most successful machines, the 123cc D1 Bantam two-stroke. Based on a prewar DKW, it was simple, cheap, worked well and sold in thousands to a transport-hungry world. During the year the M-range went over to telescopic front forks, so that BSA was now well into its postwar stride.

In 1949 plunger rear suspension became an option for the twin and the B-range, a sports twin was added as the A7 Star Twin, and the Gold Star name was revived. First offered as the 348cc B32GS, it was soon joined by a 499cc version, both based on the B-range but with an all-alloy engine, plunger frame and a massive option list. This enabled it to be set up to suit road, trial, scramble or racing use, as BSA had their eye on the Clubman's TT races.

A larger twin, the 646cc A10 Golden Flash was added for 1950, its engine similar to the A7 but revised in the light of experience, as well as enlarged. At the same time a competition version of the Bantam appeared and plunger rear suspension became an option for the Bantam, C, and M ranges. Both A7 twins were revised for 1951 so that most detail parts became common with the A10.

During 1952 BSA made another attempt to win the Maudes trophy by running three Star Twins over 5000 miles of European roads, taking in that year's ISDT en route. In this they were successful, all three riders winning a gold medal, and the firm was awarded the trophy once again.

Intended for the 1940 range, this 348cc B29 was to lead to a postwar series of new models.

In 1953 the Gold Star models moved on to pivoted-fork rear suspension, while an export-only sports A10 appeared as the Super Flash. At the other end of the scale BSA entered the cyclemotor market with their 35cc Winged Wheel which could replace any bicycle rear wheel. The firm also offered it as a complete machine, still being in the bicycle business, but the type's day was nearly over and it was dropped after three years.

After the war the C10 had a separate oil tank and, at first, continued with the girder forks.

The C11 copied the C10, both part of the 1946 range announced in August 1945.

Total Price £133. 5s.

A change of finish from khaki to black and silver allowed the M20 to go straight back into production for 1946.

Total Price £133. 5s.

The new 1946 model was the 348cc B31, destined for a long run and forerunner of several other models.

BSA COMPETITION
350 cc. Model B 32
500 cc. Model B 34

With a most impressive list of premier awards to their credit, gained in Trials and Scrambles in all parts of the world, these two B.S.A. models have proved the most successful post-war competition machines. Lucas mag-dyno lighting is standard; for alternative lighting equipment see price list. Spring frame extra (with downswept exhaust pipe only).

Above: The first of the 348cc derivatives was the competition B32, which appeared early in 1946.

BSA built an experimental twin-cylinder engine with side valves in the early postwar years. Later it was mounted in postwar cycle parts

When BSA did introduce their A7 twin for 1947, it followed conventional lines but the gearbox was bolted to the back of the crankcase.

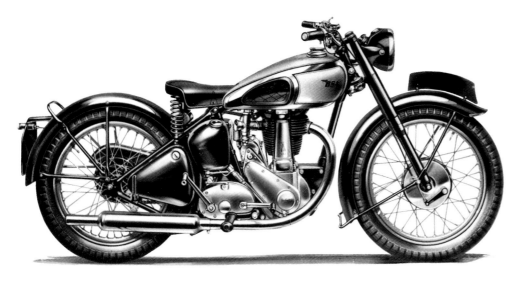

1947 brought the 499cc B33, a carbon copy of the B31.

Below: A new model for 1948 was the M33, produced by combining the B33 engine and the M-series frame.

The first Bantam, one of BSA's most successful models, which was introduced in 1948 as the 123cc D1.

Late in 1948 the M33 changed to telescopic front forks, as did the M20 and M21.

A de luxe version of the C11 in this pleasing blue was added for 1948.

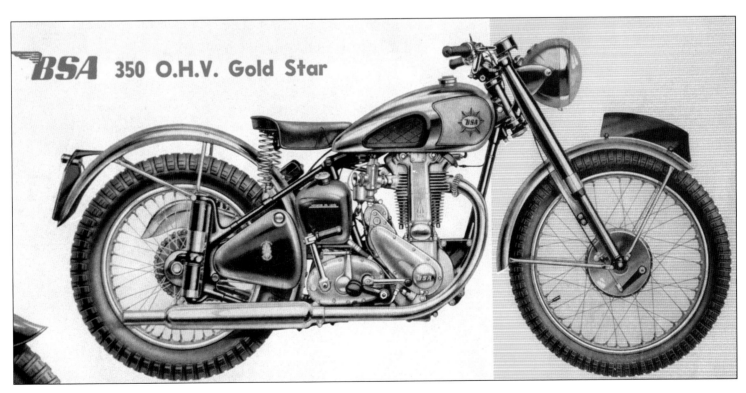

The Gold Star returned in 1949 as a sports single, targeted for competition in the Clubman's TT races which it went on to dominate. This is the 348cc ZB32GS, soon joined by a 499cc model.

Plunger rear suspension and a revised exhaust pipe line were features of the 1950 Bantam.

Plunger rear suspension and the sporting Star Twin A7ST model were introduced in 1949.

By stretching the twin to 646cc, BSA created the A10 Golden Flash
which sold more in this popular beige than the optional black.

Above: For 1951 the A7 twin had its engine revised to use parts common to the A10.

By 1953 the Gold Star had adopted pivoted-fork rear suspension to become the BB version.

The all-alloy engine was available for the competition singles from 1950, this a 1953 B34.

The BSA Super Flash

The 10 in. O.H.V. Twin cylinder motor with a power output of around 30 b.h.p.

The B.S.A. Golden Flash, introduced to American Motor Cyclists some two years ago, achieved instant popularity.

Now, from the same stable, comes the B.S.A. Super Flash—a super-duper specially tuned sports edition of the original Flash.

In design and basic specification this new Super Flash is similar to its famous forerunner, but the technical layout of the motor has been developed to produce a marked increase in power output and all-round performance. The new model retains to the full all those characteristics which make the Golden Flash so deservedly popular—flexibility, riding comfort, supreme road-holding and faultless steering.

The B.S.A. Super Flash is a must for the enthusiast who wants EVERYTHING in a motorcycle.

BSA THE MOST POPULAR MOTOR CYCLE IN THE WORLD

Top: Export-only A10 Super Flash, never seen in its own country but sold in the USA for 1953-54.

Above: A 35cc Winged Wheel fitted to a BSA cycle, but minus its magneto cover.

Left: The complete cyclemotor offered by BSA for a short time, powered by their Winged Wheel.

STABILISATION

Both the A-twin and B-single ranges received attention for 1954, becoming available in the pivoted fork frame, although the original types remained listed for a year or two, the plunger A10 remaining until 1957 to satisfy sidecar owners. Machine names and codes stayed as they were except for the sports twins which became the A7 Shooting Star and A10 Road Rocket. The competition B models went to a duplex, rigid frame for 1954, but retained the pivoted fork as an option. That year also saw the appearance of the D3 Bantam, its engine bored out to 148cc and available in the same versions of road or competition and rigid or plunger as the D1.

The C range was also altered for 1954 with a change to alternator electrics. The side-valve model adopted some Bantam cycle parts and became the C10L, which had a plunger frame; the ohv model was listed in rigid or plunger forms as the C11G. Finally, the Gold Star models had the size of their engine cooling fins increased and adopted a swept-back exhaust pipe, to be listed as the CB type.

After all this, little was changed for 1955 other than to a Monobloc carburettor for most models. Then came a simplification of the range for 1956 when the competition Bantams, Winged Wheel and M20 were dropped, and the C11G became the C12 in a pivoted-fork frame. The D3 went into a similar frame, the D1 was only listed in plunger form, and there were fewer alternatives throughout the range.

Two new models were shown as BSA attempted to join the scooter market. One, the 200cc Beeza, failed to go into production, but the other, the 70cc Dandy scooterette did, but not until 1957. The end of that year saw the range contract further as the C10L, B32, B34 and M33 were dropped from the lists.

For 1958 the D3 Bantam was enlarged to become the 172cc D5 and the sports A10 became the Super Rocket. It was joined by the export-only Rocket Scrambler, which was sold in the USA as a street scrambler with open pipes, no lights and off-road fittings and was listed as the Spitfire from 1960.

Opposite: Plunger rear suspension remained listed for the A10 up to 1957, and was preferred by many sidecar drivers.

Below: Golden Flash A10 in the pivoted-fork frame used from 1954, its use requiring a separate gearbox to be fitted.

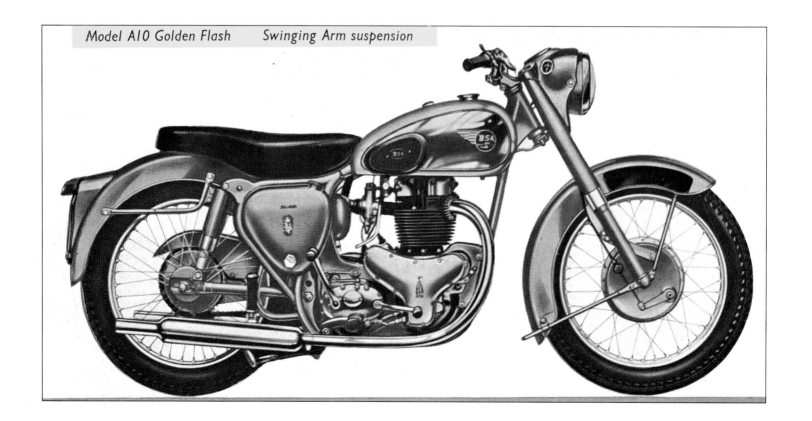

Model A10 Golden Flash   Swinging Arm suspension

SPRING-TIME *you had a*

The B.S.A. Golden Flash is a good-looker—and its performance and comfort are every bit as good as its appearance suggests. The 650 O.H.V. Twin engine has all the power and flexibility you could wish for, and is remarkably silent; the 4-speed gearbox is smooth and easy in operation, whilst the duplex frame design gives complete riding comfort, hairline steering and perfect road-holding. The "Bantam" is the 'go-anywhere' machine that made low-cost motor-cycling popular.

BSA WINNERS OF THE MAUDES TROPHY

BSA

THE MOST POPULAR MOTOR CYCLE IN THE WORLD

B-range singles in the new frame, first seen on the Gold Star, and in their 1955 maroon finish.

The sports 499cc twin became the A7SS Shooting Star in the new frame, one of the smoothest of the BSA twins.

The sports twin was the A10RR Road Rocket which used the Super Flash engine in the new frame. This is a 1957 version for the USA.

For 1954 the competition singles went into a duplex rigid frame.

Pivoted-fork rear suspension remained available for the B32 and B34 competition singles.

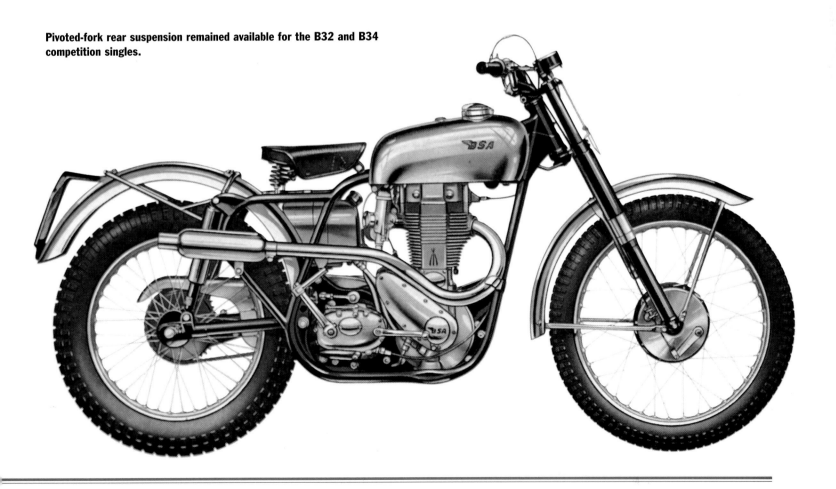

A larger, 148cc D3 Bantam Major appeared for 1954, similar to the D1 but with heavier front forks.

Alternator electrics were introduced to the C-range in 1954, the side-valve model becoming the C10L using Bantam forks and wheels.

The ohv model became the C11G, available in rigid or plunger form with three or four speeds.

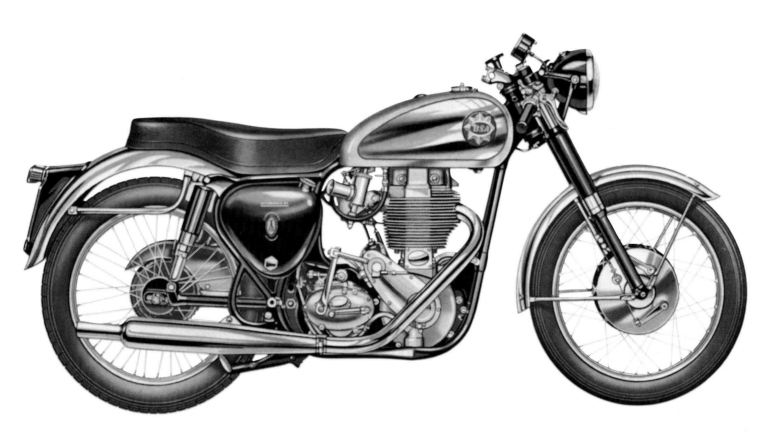

By 1954 the Gold Star had become the CB type with much deeper engine fins and a swept-back exhaust system.

Fitting the C11G engine into a pivoted-fork frame produced the C12 for 1956.

For 1956 the D3 Bantam had a pivoted-fork frame, while the D1 continued in plunger form only.

In the USA the B34 was sold as the 'Alloy Clipper' but was the same as the home market version.

Dandy scooterette which had an awkward two-speed preselector gearbox and its ignition points buried in the middle of the engine unit. Public and trade disliked both features.

The Beeza scooter which was exhibited at the Earls Court show late in 1955 but never went into production.

The M33 in its final 1957 year, after which its job was taken over by other models.

In 1958 the D5 Bantam was created by enlarging the engine to 172cc while keeping the D3 cycle parts.

The larger sports twin became the Super Rocket in 1958, this the USA version with raised bars.

Below: Export only Spitfire Scrambler sold in the USA from 1958 to 1963.

UNIT SINGLES

ate in 1958 BSA launched the first of a new series of unit-construction singles, the 247cc C15. Based on the design of the Triumph Tiger Cub, it had a vertical cylinder, unit construction and up-to-date lines. Its appearance in the 1959 programme meant that the C12 was dropped, while the D5 became the D7, still of 172cc but in a new frame with better forks and styling changes. Early in 1959 the new 250 was joined by two competition versions, the C15S for scrambles and the C15T for trials, both modified to suit their off-road purposes.

The group had another attempt at the scooter market in 1959, offering two models, each available as a BSA-Sunbeam or as a Triumph by changing colour and badges. Virtually identical in most respects, the models differed in having either a Bantam-based, 172cc, two-stroke engine, or a new 249cc ohv twin. Both had a four-speed gearbox based on that used by the Triumph Cub and the new C15 and neither was a success. The twin did reach the shops in 1959, but the single took until 1960, and few were sold.

At the end of 1959 the long-serving B31 was dropped, the B33 going a year later. The M21 became available to special order only, selling mainly to the AA and the services. The Gold Star machines were only built in Clubman or scrambles form, their TT races having ceased after 1956 by which time BSA had come to dominate them.

The start of the new decade saw the British industry celebrating 1959 as its best year ever, but it was at the beginning of a long decline. BSA kept to their range, but began to expand the unit-single line in 1961, when they added the 247cc super-sports SS80 and the 343cc B40, a bored-out C15. This was joined by the 343cc SS90 for 1962, similar to the SS80, but time was to show that these high-compression sports singles could be fragile if abused.

Late in 1958 BSA introduced their first unit single, the 247cc C15, which led to a whole series of models.

with the **NEW** 250 cc STAR

£172 including £34.2.6 purchase tax

There were three more twins for 1962, but all, even the two supposedly new ones, had their roots in the past. The charismatic twin was the A10RGS, known as the Rocket Gold Star. First conceived by Gold Star specialist Eddie Dow, who fitted a sports twin engine into a Goldie frame for a customer, it could have been done by using nearly all stock parts. However, BSA used a number of special parts and the result was an outstanding machine. Built for just two years, it was the final sports form of the A10 series. The A10, Super Rocket and Spitfire continued with it until 1963, but the two A7 models were dropped a year earlier.

The 172cc Bantam became the D7 for 1959, with an improved frame and forks.

Early 1959 saw the introduction of competition versions of the unit single, this the C15S scrambles model.

Another attempt at the scooter market brought this BSA-Sunbeam model, also sold as a Triumph.

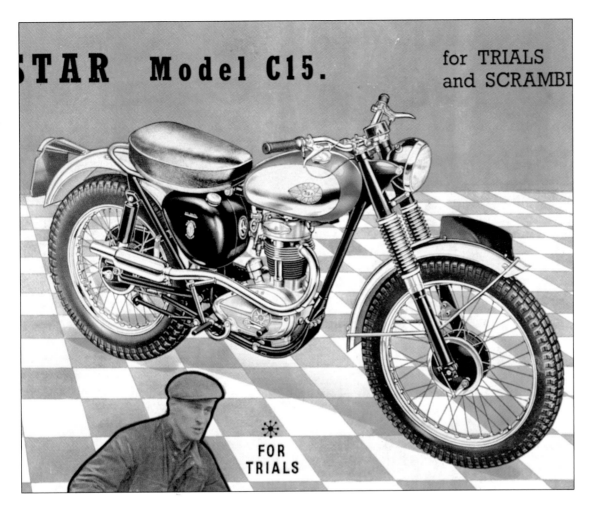

STAR Model C15. for TRIALS and SCRAMB[LING]

FOR TRIALS

For the trials enthusiast, BSA listed the C15T, both it and the C15S much as the road one.

Well restored M-range side-valve single from the 1956-57 period.

The AA used the M21 to haul its distinctive yellow outfits for many years, a welcome sight to many a motorist in trouble.

Late type DBD Gold Star in road trim for the USA, hence the high bars. The machine was listed as the 'Road Racer'.

The final version of the B33 appeared in 1960 - a good machine but the times demanded more sporting attributes.

In 1961 the 247cc Sport Star SS80 joined the C15, as a result of the law restricting learner riders to that capacity.

At home the road-going Gold Star was only sold in the highly popular Clubman's trim.

In scrambles trim the Gold Star took a strong man to get the best from it and was superseded by the C15S which was less spectacular but faster.

The 1961 343cc B40, essentially a bored-out C15, would have been more suited to learners' needs.

A year later, the 343cc SS90 Sports Star joined the ranks of unit singles to offer more performance.

The fabulous Rocket Gold Star was only offered for 1962-63, but became a classic, and for many the greatest of the A10 series.

The last year for the Super Rocket was 1963 and many were fitted with the options to give the looks of the Rocket Gold Star.

The A7 was dropped after 1962, along with the A7SS. Both had served riders well for more than a decade.

UNIT TWINS

The two new twins introduced for 1962 were intended to replace the old. Listed as the 499cc A50 and 654cc A65, they had unit construction of ohv engine and four-speed gearbox, nearly all parts common, and less weight than the earlier twins. However, much of the internal design, if not the parts, was unchanged, although there was a move to alternator electrics and coil ignition. Unfortunately, although actually lighter, they had a heavy bulbous look that failed to interest or excite buyers as the old Golden Flash or Shooting Star had.

The Dandy and the 348cc Gold Star were dropped at the end of 1962, and the larger Gold Star a year later. Other models that went after 1963 were the much-loved D1 Bantam (a bad move), the M21, as the AA turned to small vans, and the A10 twins, including the stylish and highly desirable Rocket Gold Star.

New for 1963 was the export-only C15 Pastoral built for trail use and joined for 1964 by the larger B40E Enduro Star. Also new that year was the 75cc Beagle, intended as a starter model and fitted with an ohv engine also used in reduced 50cc capacity form by the Ariel Pixie. The style of the Beagle was rather dated, along the lines of a 1950s moped, and it was not a success.

In the twin range for 1964 there were five new models, four of them export only. For home use there was the A65R Rocket, which had a tuned engine and brighter finish, the export version being the A65T/R Thunderbolt Rocket styled for the USA. Fitted with twin carburettors and a cylinder head with splayed inlet ports, it became the A65L/R Lightning Rocket, while the other two machines were for off-road use. Both had twin carburettors, open exhausts and no lights, and were listed as the A50CC Cyclone Competition and A65SH Spitfire Hornet.

At the end of 1964 BSA gave up with the 249cc scooter, the smaller version going soon after in 1965. That year the singles ran on as they were with one important addition, the 441cc B44GP Grand Prix built solely for moto-cross. Based firmly on

The smaller of the new twins for 1962 was the 499cc A50 Star, which had unit construction and much that was derived from the older twins.

the machines used by works rider Jeff Smith to win the world title in 1964 and 1965, it had many special parts fitted to it.

The twin range became confused for 1965, despite the A65T/R being dropped. The three home market and the other three export models all continued, and were joined by five more, four for home buyers. These four were the A50C Cyclone and A65L Lightning sports models plus the A50CC Cyclone Clubman and A65LC Lightning Clubman which were set up for production racing so could be fitted out from a long list of options. The new export model was another A50C, this time a Cyclone Roadster for the USA.

The larger new twin was the 654cc A65 Star, which was impossible to distinguish from the smaller one other than by colour and markings.

The 1964 B40E Enduro Star built for export to the USA for trail riding and based on the C15T chassis.

BSA Beagle, a 75cc ohv starter-model which had dated lines and did not prove popular.

A sports version of the new twin appeared on the home market for 1964 as the A65R Rocket, with a tuned engine and brighter finish.

In the USA the 1964 sports twin became the A65T/R
Thunderbolt Rocket with high bars.

The twin-carburettor version of the 1964 USA twin was the
A65L/R Lightning Rocket.

For off-road trail or enduro use in the USA there was the
A50CC Cyclone Competition in 1964.

NEW PRICE £354.13.7 (including £62.9.7 P.T. which includes 10% surcharge)

BSA Victor Grand Prix Model B44 GP. Price £349 (including £56.16.0 PT)

Manufacturers recommended retail price

Polished alloy guards

Fibre-glass air cleaner with double paper element

Light alloy cylinder with hard chrome plated bore

Oil filler

Light alloy petrol tank

Chrome molybdenum fork shafts

Hydraulically-damped suspension units, adjustable for load

Frame of Reynolds 531 tubing w reinforced head-lug
Oil carried i frame tubes integral header tank

7 in. rear brake

New inter damping u

Q.D. wheels, front and rear

7 in. front br

Upswept exhaust system with megaphone

Oil header tank

Ground clearance 7 in. (laden)

Contact breaker with automatic ignition control mounted in timing case and driven from camshaft

Specially strengthened crankcase with heavy-duty roller bearings drive side and ball bearings on

This is the 1967 version of the B44GP Victor Grand Prix which was built for moto-cross use and based on the championship-winning works machines.

The larger trail twin was the A65SH Spitfire Hornet, again with high level, open pipes.

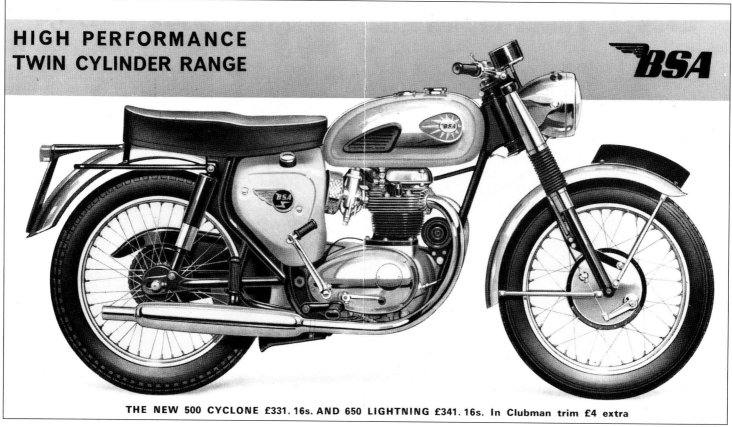

HIGH PERFORMANCE TWIN CYLINDER RANGE

BSA

THE NEW 500 CYCLONE £331. 16s. AND 650 LIGHTNING £341. 16s. In Clubman trim £4 extra

At home the A50C Cyclone and A65L Lightning became the super-sports models for 1965, both with twin carburettors.

For production-machine racing both twins were available in a highly tuned form, this being the larger A65LC Lightning Clubman.

In the USA the A50C Cyclone Roadster was listed for 1965, with the tuned, twin-carburettor engine.

RANGE REVAMP

All this trauma and confusion was swept away for 1966 when virtually the whole range was given a new coding, only the basic C15 and special B44GP continuing as they were. Out went the rest, many for good, and those that stayed had changes. The Beagle was not among them, so the smallest model became the D7 Bantam, offered as the Silver, an economy model, and the De Luxe. Next came the C15, and its sports counterpart the C15 Sportsman, which replaced the SS80. There were no 343cc models, and the next size machine was the 441cc B44VE Victor Enduro, which used a detuned B44GP engine in a C15 competition frame.

The twin range was reduced to six models. The basic road machines became the A50R Royal Star and A65T Thunderbolt. The sports model was the A65L Lightning, and for production racing the A65LC was replaced by the A65SS Spitfire MkII. It was highly tuned and fast, but fragile. For off-road use BSA continued to list two engine sizes as the A50W Wasp and A65H Hornet, which had options on exhaust systems, silencers, tyres, tanks and undershield.

During 1966 the Bantam became the D10 type with more power, a better generator, and the contact points moved over to the right where they sat on the outside of the primary chaincase under a small cover. Four D10 Bantams were listed, the Silver and Supreme much as the D7, but the others graduated to a much-needed four-speed gearbox. The first was the Sports, which had a waist-level exhaust system, humped seat and flyscreen, the other the Bushman, which was built for trail use with suitable tyres and gearing.

For 1966 the D10 Bantam was offered in four forms. This is the economy Silver version.

The D10 models continued for 1967 along with the twins, the A65 Spitfire becom-

ing the MkIII model. Of the unit singles, the C15 had a much stronger bottom end fitted and was joined by the C25 Barracuda which replaced the C15 Sportsman. This was a super-sports machine which had a square-fin barrel and different engine internals, although it kept to the C15 concept. It was sold in the USA as the B25 Starfire and a 441cc version was built as the B44VR Victor Roadster, similar in looks but different internally. With it came the B44VS Victor Special produced as a trail model with suitable wheels, tyres, gearing, headlight and exhaust system.

There were further deletions and additions for 1968, the Bantams becoming the D14/4 Supreme, D14/4S Sports and D14/4B Bushman models, all with the four-speed gearbox. The C15 finally went, as did the B44GP, B44VE and C25, only the B25 being listed, while the 441cc road model became the B44SS Shooting Star, the B44VS running on as it was. Of the twins the A50W was dropped, the Spitfire became the MkIV, and the A65H became the A65FS Firebird Scrambler.

The Sports D10S had a much-needed four-speed gearbox along with its sports styling features.

In 1966 the sports 247cc model became the C15 Sportsman, fitted with a humped seat.

Sports A65L Lightning twin for the 1967 USA season, twin carburettors being a standard fitment.

The basic smaller twin for 1966 was the A50R Royal Star, here in 1967 USA form.

For production racing BSA listed the Spitfire A65SS. This is the MkII form seen in 1966.

During 1966 the Bantam became the D10, still of 172cc, but available in four forms, this being the Supreme, which was much as the D7 De Luxe.

The smaller off-road model became the A50W Wasp for 1966. This one is fitted with low-level silencers.

For 1967 the A65SS Spitfire took on a MkIII form, losing its Grand Prix carburettors in the process.

The larger off-road machine was the A65H Hornet. This is the 1967 version.

Trail Bantam riders could choose the D10B Bushman which was modified to suit its purpose. This is a later 1969 version of the type.

Revised for 1967, the 247cc C25 Barracuda had a one-piece crankshaft and a crankcase based on that of the Victor Grand Prix.

BSA STARFIRE 250 250cc (15 cu. in.) Single

In the USA the C25 was sold as the B25 Starfire, and this name was also used on the home market from 1968.

The 1968 Bantam models continued at 172cc but took D14 codes and all had a four-speed gearbox. This is the D14/4 Supreme, the base version.

The sports version of the 1968 Bantam range was this D14/4S with humped seat and flyscreen.

The trail version of the unit single was this B44VS Victor Special, the internals of the larger engine differing from the smaller.

BSA SHOOTING STAR 441 441cc Alloy Single

Launched as the B44VR Victor Roadster and fitted with a 441cc version of the revised unit single engine,
this model became the B44SS Shooting Star for 1968.

BSA SPITFIRE MARK IV SPECIAL 650cc (40 cu. in.) Twin dual car

The last year for the A65SS Spitfire was 1968, when it took its MkIV form. This is the USA version.

BSA FIREBIRD SCRAMBLER 650cc (40 cu. in.) Twin with dual carburetors

Off-road, the twin became the A65FS Firebird Scrambler with high-level pipes and full road equipment.

For 1969 the Firebird Scrambler moved both exhaust systems to the left, resulting in a better line.

ROCKET 3

A new and special machine joined the 1968 range, and was introduced to press and public in March that year as the A75 Rocket 3, along with the similar Triumph T150 Trident. Both had a 740cc three-cylinder engine set across the frame and in unit with a four-speed gearbox. Although many of the internals were common, and the design owed much to the Triumph twin, the BSA was distinguished by having its cylinders inclined forward and its timing cover shaped to blend to the gearbox one.

The frames also differed, following the lines of the two firms' respective twins, so that the BSA had an all-welded type with duplex downtubes. The forks and wheels were common and taken from the twin, the front brake of the twin-leading-shoe type. A four-gallon tank was fitted, with an oil cooler mounted beneath it at the front.

It was a most impressive motorcycle which reached its home market in 1969 and soon built up a fine reputation. Unfortunately, its production had been delayed, and late in 1968 the Honda CB750 burst onto the scene to steal much of the triple's thunder. For all that, the British machines sold well and works racing versions had considerable success in 1970 and 1971, winning at Daytona, the TT, the Bol d'Or and Thruxton.

With the advent of the triple, the Spitfire was dropped for 1969, while the Bantam had its engine modified considerably to become the D175 in road and Bushman forms. The only addition to the range was the B25 Fleetstar, a low-cost version for fleet buyers. It was only listed for the one year, but the rest of the range ran on until 1970, when major changes were announced.

The 740cc Rocket 3, A75, triple was launched in 1968 along with the similar Triumph Trident. Fine machines that performed well given correct maintenance.

The other side of the Rocket 3 was just as impressive as the first, the 'ray-gun' silencer outlets a noted feature.

This picture comes from the USA brochure for the early Rocket 3.

The final Bantam was the 1969 D175, whose engine was modified in detail, the central sparking plug a long awaited improvement

The low-cost B25 Fleetstar was offered for bulk buyers in 1969, but was seldom seen. This one was sighted in 1993.

NEW RANGE

Late in 1970 BSA and Triumph staged a massive trade and press launch of their 1971 models. There were both new and heavily revised machines, few escaping without some change. Much became common across the marques and their models; the same forks, wheels and many fittings were used for one and all. Only the Bantam was left alone, listed in road form only.

Five unit singles were listed, the engines continuing the series theme, but the frames, forks, wheels and style were all new. Two were of 247cc, one the B25SS Gold Star 250 Street Scrambler, the other the B25T Victor 250 Trail. Both carried their engine oil within the frame and had conical hubs, as did all the singles and twins. The larger models were of 499cc and listed as the B50SS Gold Star 500 Street Scrambler, the B50T Victor 500 Trail and the B50MX Victor 500 Moto-cross. The use of the revered Gold Star name was far from popular with BSA owners and it was an indication as to how far the firm had drifted from its prosperous roots.

Of the twins, only the three larger continued as the A65T, A65L and A65FS, but in new, oil-bearing frames fitted with the new group forks carrying the wheels with conical hubs. The new front brake lacked the bite of the old and even appeared on the Rocket 3 despite that model's weight and speed. It too was restyled to have a small fuel tank and all the frames were finished in a light dove grey that showed grime instantly.

One further twin was shown at the launch. This was of 349cc and had twin overhead camshafts. Built as both BSA and Triumph marques, it was listed as the E35R Fury and E35SS Fury SS in road and street scrambler forms. While the engine and its five-speed gearbox were all new, the forks and wheels were group parts along with other details.

The short-lived 1971 B25SS, or Gold Star 250 Street Scrambler as BSA chose to call it.

So many changes at once placed far too great a burden on a group already in financial deep water. As a result, the two new E35 twins did not go into production, for the factory had many other problems to cope with, not the least being the excessive seat height of the new frame used by both marques of twins.

The outcome was inevitable. The range shrank for 1972, the Bantam and both 250s being dropped, along with the A65FS. This left the three 499cc singles, two 654cc twins and the triple, all of which now had a black finish for their frame. An additional triple, the A75V, with a five-speed gearbox, was listed and a batch of larger twins was built for the USA to take advantage of the capacity limits for their racing. They were stretched out to 751cc and listed as the A70L, and a few remained in Britain. In the USA they were sometimes referred to as the Lightning 75.

The 1971 B25T Victor 250 Trail model, not much different from the other 247cc single and no more popular.

Below left: The 499cc road unit single of 1971 had the equally cumbersome title of B50SS Gold Star 500 Street Scrambler, but did qualify for a bigger front brake.

Below right: The B50T Victor 500 Trail model copied the other 1971 unit singles in its construction.

For scramblers the unit single was offered as the B50MX Victor 500 Moto-Cross and was later developed into the CCM range of machines.

Base 1971 twin was the A65T Thunderbolt in the new oil-bearing frame, famed for its excessive height.

The 1971 twin-carburettor A65L Lightning was very similar to the Thunderbolt, sharing most parts.

The A65FS continued with the high level pipes on the left, but was otherwise much as the other twins.

One of a pair of twins which was not destined to reach production in 1971 was this 349cc E35R Fury which had twin overhead camshafts and a five-speed gearbox.

That light dove grey 1971 frame finish used on the twins and this Rocket 3 showed road dirt as soon as the machines turned a wheel, and, consequently, was soon dropped.

The Fury SS E35SS model of 1971 which had high level pipes to distinguish it. The finish was listed as 'Plum Crazy'.

1972 was the last year for real BSA machines, and this is the best of them, the highly-regarded Rocket 3.

END – AND AFTER

T hen it was all over. The great BSA company went down, a victim of its latter-
day decisions and earlier procrastination. The B50MX lingered for a year, and
the engine was later developed and used in the CCM. A T65 Thunderbolt was
seen in 1973, but it was really a Triumph TR6 with BSA badges.

Although the Small Heath factory was torn down, the name lived on to be seen
again on a series of mopeds and small motorcycles. All were assembled using mainly imported parts and in this way the company continues to this day. However, for
BSA enthusiasts the end came in 1972 and it is the memory of the years before that
should be preserved. The years when BSA dominated trials, scrambles, Clubman's
TT racing and, above all, built good motorcycles.

Beaver was one of a series of 50cc models
which shared many components, being the
basic roadster.

Easy Rider mopeds were first offered by NVT and were available in single or two-speed forms, the latter working well.

Tracker models were available in 125 and 175cc sizes, had a six-speed gearbox and off-road style.

This Junior off-road fun bike for the young used the Easy Rider engine unit.

Above: The Boxer had a little more power, so could be offered as a sports moped, set off by its own paint finish.

For off-road style BSA listed the Brigand, with a raised exhaust and trail mudguards.

BSA MODEL LIST

These are arranged by capacity, number of cylinders, engine type and years that this combination was used. The code was that used to identify the model but all given may not have been built for all years.

cc	Cyl	Type	Year	Code
35	1	t/s	1953-55	WW
70	1	t/s	1957-62	Dandy
75	1	ohv	1964-65	K1 Beagle
123	1	t/s	1948-63	D1
148	1	t/s	1954-57	D3
149	1	ohv	1934-36	X
172	1	t/s	1958-71	D5, D7, D,10, D14, D175, B1
174	1	t/s	1928-30	A
247	1	ohv	1958-71	C15, C15S, C15T, C15P, SS80, C15Sp, C25, B25, B25SS, B25T
249	1	sv	1924-57	B, B20, C10, C10L
249	1	ohv	1930-58	B, B21, B22, C11, C11G, C12
249	2	ohv	1959-64	B2, B2S
343	1	ohv	1961-67	B40, SS90, B40E
348	1	sv	1923-40	L, B23, C12
348	1	ohv	1924-62	L, R, B24, B25, B26, B29, M19, B31, B32, B32GS
441	1	ohv	1965-70	B44GP, B44VE, B44VS, B44VR, B44SS
493	1	sv	1923-31	S
493	1	ohv	1927-32	S
495	2	ohv	1947-50	A7, A7ST
496	1	sv	1937-55	M20
496	1	ohv	1937-40	M22, M23 M24
497	2	ohv	1951-62	A7, A7ST, A7SS
499	1	sv	1911-20	A,D
499	1	sv	1932-36	W
499	1	ohv	1932-63	W, Q, B33, B34, B34GS, M33
499	1	ohv	1971-73	B50SS, B50T, B50MX
499	2	ohv	1934-36	J
499	2	ohv	1962-70	A50, A50C, A50CC, A50W
556	1	sv	1914-32	H, K
591	1	sv	1938-63	M21
596	1	sv	1933-37	M, M21
596	1	ohv	1933-35	M
646	2	ohv	1950-63	A10, A10SF, A10RR, A10SR, A10Sp, A10RGS
654	2	ohv	1962-72	A65, A65T, A65R, A65T/R, A65LC, A65L/R, A65SS, A65L, A65SH, A65H, A65FS
740	3	ohv	1968-72	A75, A75V
748	2	ohv	1936-38	Y
751	2	ohv	1972	A70L
771	2	sv	1920-31	E
985	2	sv	1922-40	F, G